curiou?about

CODING WITH RASPBERRY PI

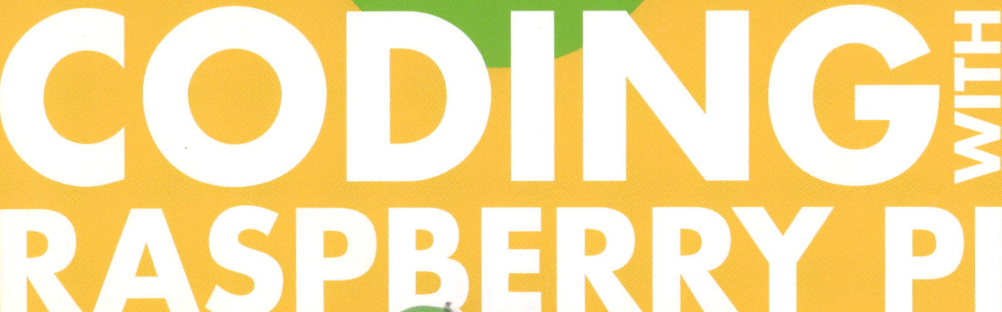

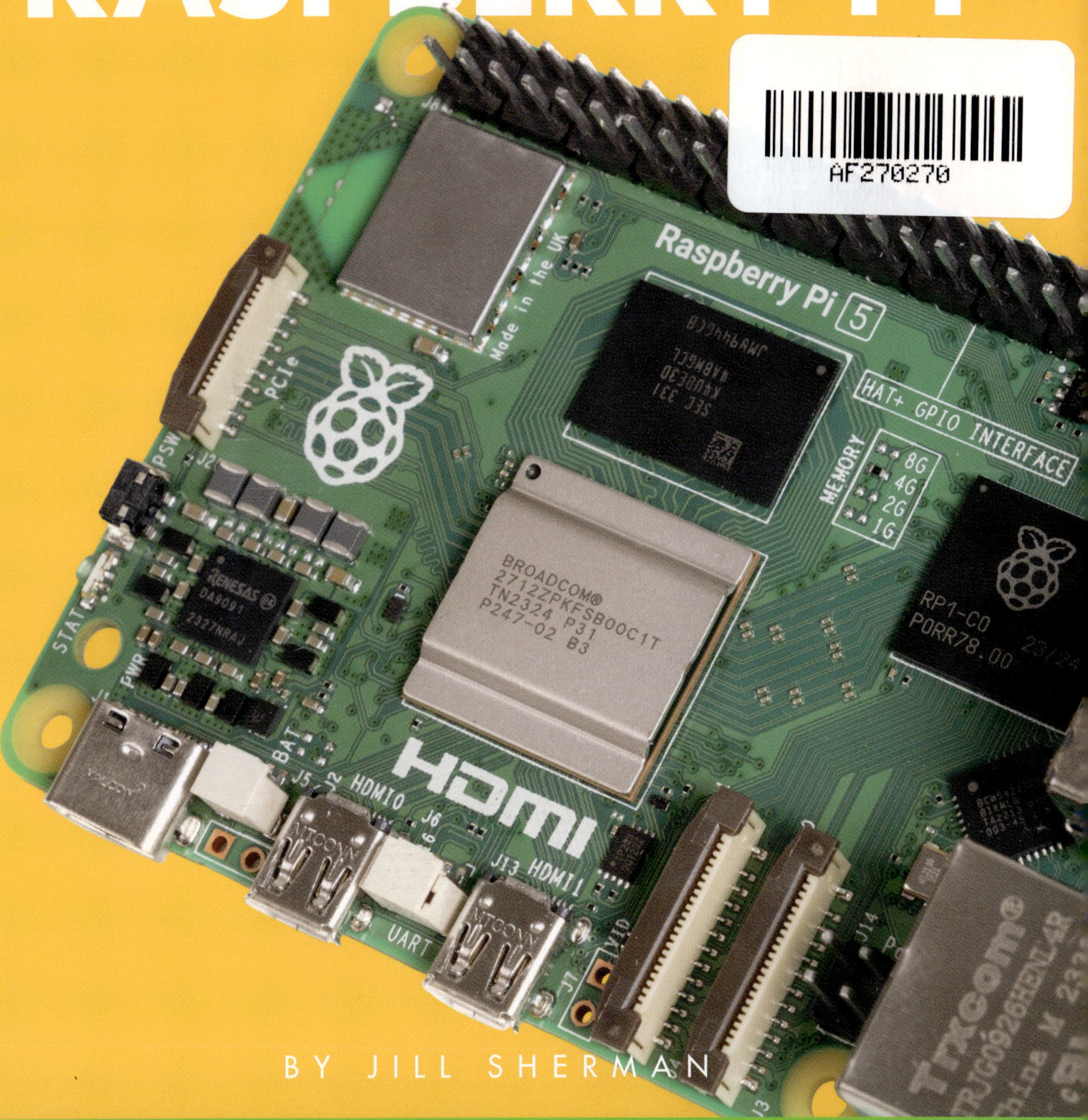

BY JILL SHERMAN

AMICUS LEARNING

What are you

CHAPTER TWO

2

Building Out

PAGE

12

CHAPTER ONE

1

Up and Running

PAGE

4

curious about?

CHAPTER THREE

3

Thinking Forward
PAGE
18

Stay Curious! Learn More . . .22

Glossary. 24

Index 24

Curious About is published by
Amicus Learning, an imprint of Amicus
P.O. Box 227, Mankato, MN 56002
www.amicuspublishing.us

Editor: Ana Brauer
Series Designer: Kathleen Petelinsek
Book Designer and Photo Researcher: Emily Dietz

Library of Congress Cataloging-in-Publication Data
Names: Sherman, Jill, author.
Title: Curious about coding with Raspberry Pi / by Jill Sherman.
Description: Mankato, MN : Amicus Learning, an imprint of
Amicus [2026] | Series: Curious about coding | Includes
bibliographical references and index. | Audience: Ages 6–9
| Audience: Grades 2–3 | Summary: "What is Raspberry Pi
and how do I use it? Learn about coding and programming with
Raspberry Pi in this question-and-answer book for elementary
readers. Includes table of contents, glossary, books and websites
for further research, and index"— Provided by publisher.
Identifiers: LCCN 2024048328 (print) | LCCN 2024048329
(ebook) | ISBN 9798892004985 (library binding) | ISBN
9798892005524 (paperback) | ISBN 9798892006064 (ebook)
Subjects: LCSH: Raspberry Pi (Computer)—Programming—
Juvenile literature. | Raspberry Pi (Computer)—Miscellanea.
| Microcomputers—Programming—Juvenile literature. |
Python (Computer program language)—Juvenile literature.
Classification: LCC QA76.8.R15 S494 2026 (print) | LCC
QA76.8.R15 (ebook) | DDC 005.265—dc23/eng/20250102
LC record available at https://lccn.loc.gov/2024048328
LC ebook record available at https://lccn.loc.gov/2024048329

Photo Credits: Alamy Stock Photo/mediasculp, 2, 12–13; Getty
Images/Anthony Harvey, 7; NASA/Jack Danos, 17; Shutterstock/
Bogdan Vija, 3, 19, Daniel Chetroni, 20–21, Golubovy, 8–9,
huntingSHARK, 15, myboys.me, 10, Rawpixel.com, 5, 16, Vas_
Kondr, 6, y0ye, cover, 1, 2, 4; The Noun Project/ ainul muttaqin,
15 (mouse), Anwar Hossain, 15 (keyboard), Daniel Chmielarczyk,
22, 23, DesignBite, 22, 23, Dwi Budiyanto, 15 (ethernet), ims.
icon, 15 (memory card), Kosong Tujuh, 15 (headphones), Majide,
15 (computer monitor), Shane Willis, 15 (USB); Wikimedia
Commons/Clem Rutter, Rochester, Kent, 11, Jeff Geerling, 14

Every effort has been made to contact copyright holders for
material reproduced in this book. Any omissions will be rectified
in subsequent printings if notice is given to the publisher.

Printed in India

What is Raspberry Pi?

Raspberry Pi 5 was released in October 2023.

Well, it's not a dessert! The Raspberry Pi is a small computer. It's only as big as a library card. It is low cost and good for coding. This makes it a great learning tool.

Raspberry Pi is often used to learn
about computers and coding.

Who made it?

Eben Upton taught about computers at St. John's College in Cambridge, England. He saw many students were good at coding. But they didn't know much about computer **hardware**. His solution? A **hobby computer**! These computers are cheap, small, and easy to use.

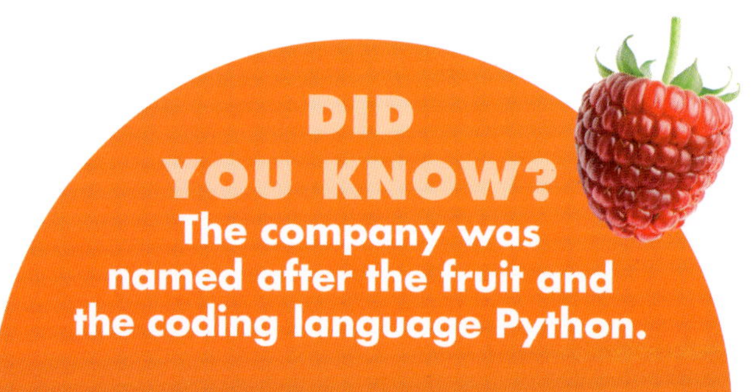

Eben Upton released
the first Raspberry
Pi in 2012.

Is it like a regular computer?

The **motherboard** contains all the circuits and connections needed to run a computer.

Kind of! If you took apart your computer, you would see that every part connects to a motherboard. With Raspberry Pi, it's all in one. It IS a motherboard, but better! All the parts are built in.

How does Raspberry Pi work?

Raspberry Pi lets you level up your electronics projects. Maybe you made a laser pointer. With Raspberry Pi, you could make a security system. Write code to give your device instructions. If the laser beam is broken, Raspberry Pi can tell your device to buzz.

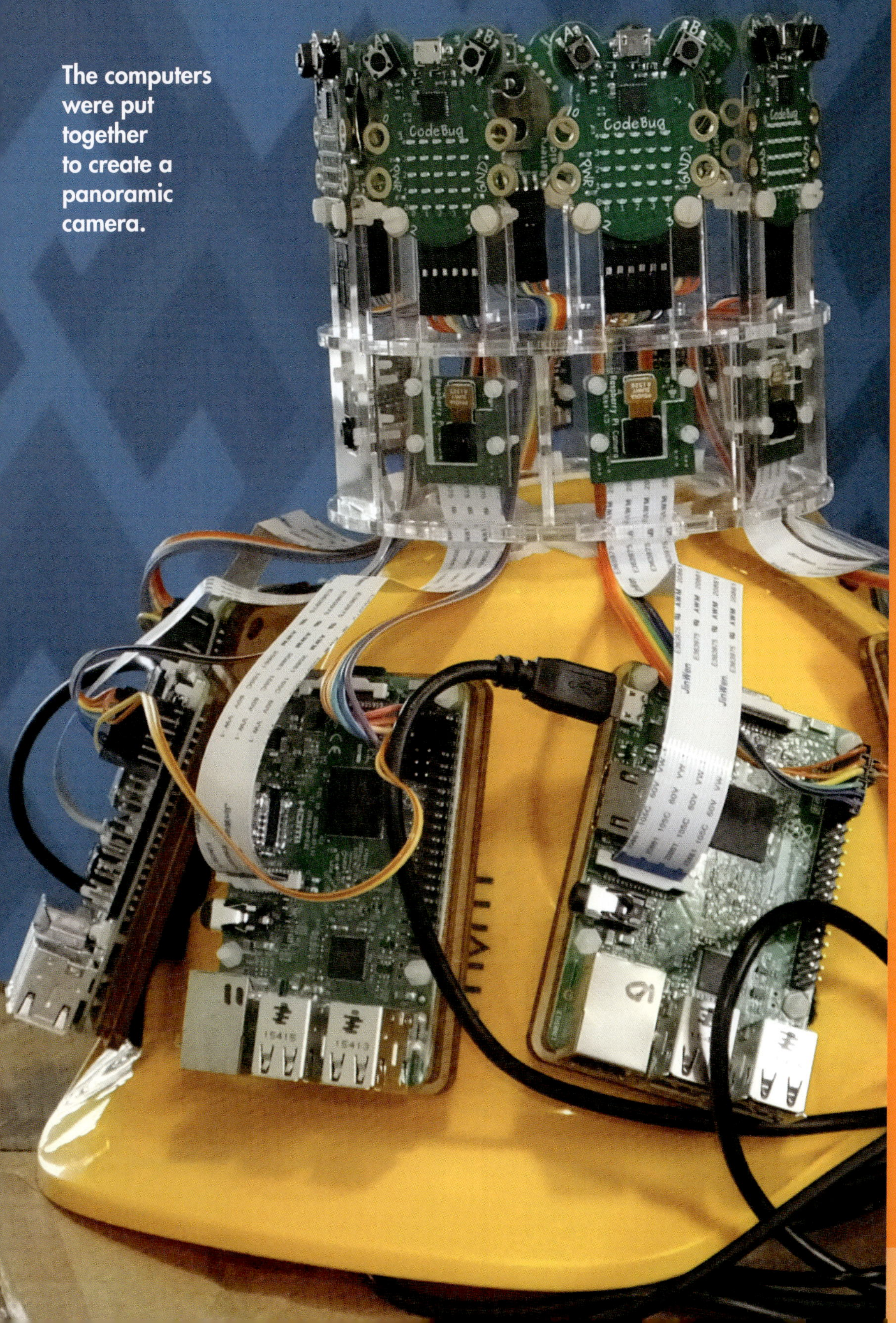

The computers were put together to create a panoramic camera.

CHAPTER TWO

How do I use a Raspberry Pi?

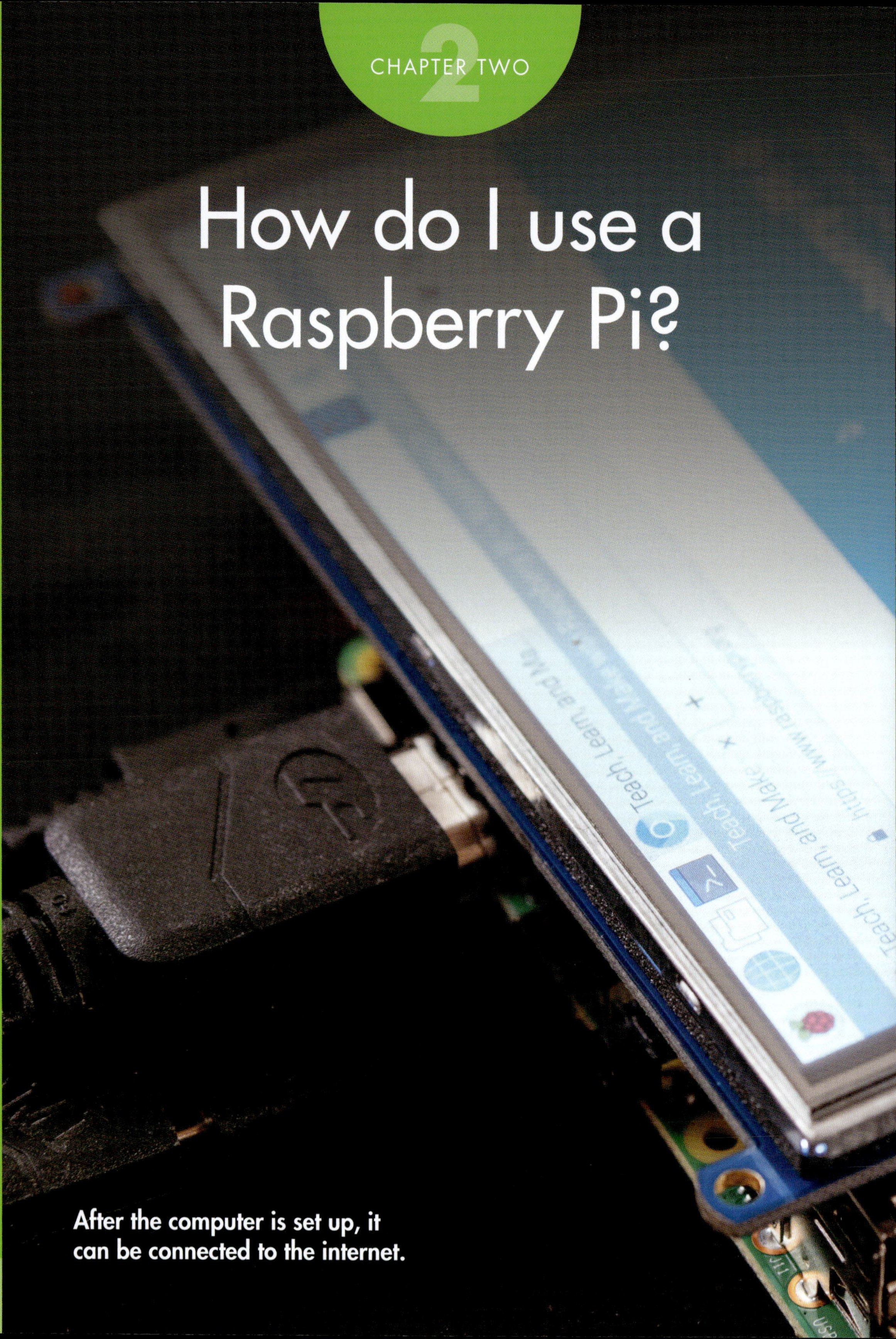

After the computer is set up, it can be connected to the internet.

Connect the device to some hardware, such as a monitor. Then set up an operating system (OS). This is the basic software that controls a computer. Raspberry Pi primarily uses Raspberry Pi OS.

Connecting a lens can turn your computer into a camera.

What connects to it?

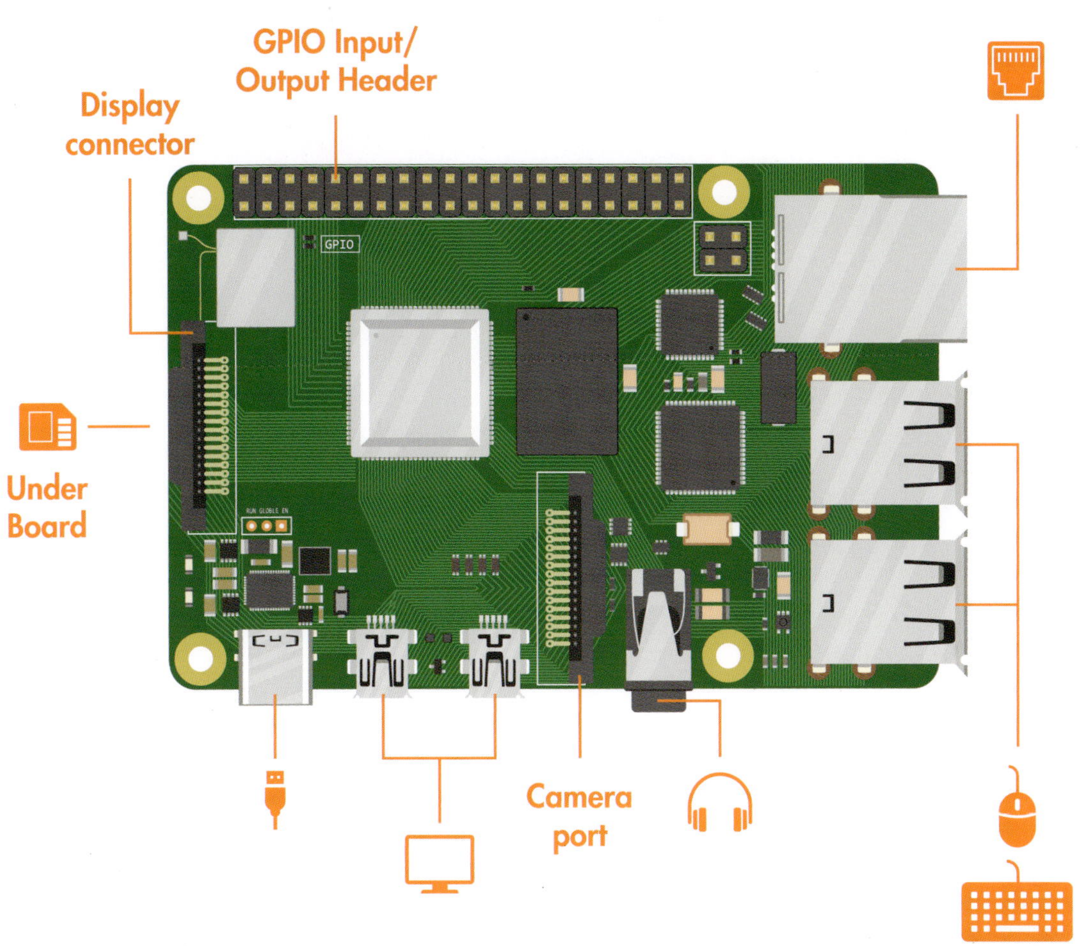

To build a device you need more than just the computer. Raspberry Pi has a camera port. Just plug in a camera. Then your device can take photo, video, or sense motion. It also has **General Purpose Input/Output (GPIO)** pins. These pins can connect to buttons, **LEDs**, or sensors.

What can I build with Raspberry Pi?

A teacher can help you build and code your computer.

So many things! Attach LEDs and make a night-light that turns itself on and off. Add speakers and use them to play music. Or you can make and program your own robot. The only limit is your imagination!

This satellite was the first time a Raspberry Pi was used as an onboard computer.

DID YOU KNOW?

In 2022, students at Utah State University used Raspberry Pi as the computer for a small satellite. It spent 117 days in space and sent back photos.

CHAPTER THREE

Why make something you can buy?

Lots of reasons! You could save some money by making it yourself. You also learn a lot when you make something new. You could even personalize your device. Fit it to your lunch box. Or make it wearable! It can be whatever you want.

Your device could
be used to create a
computer controlled car.

Will there be a new Raspberry Pi?

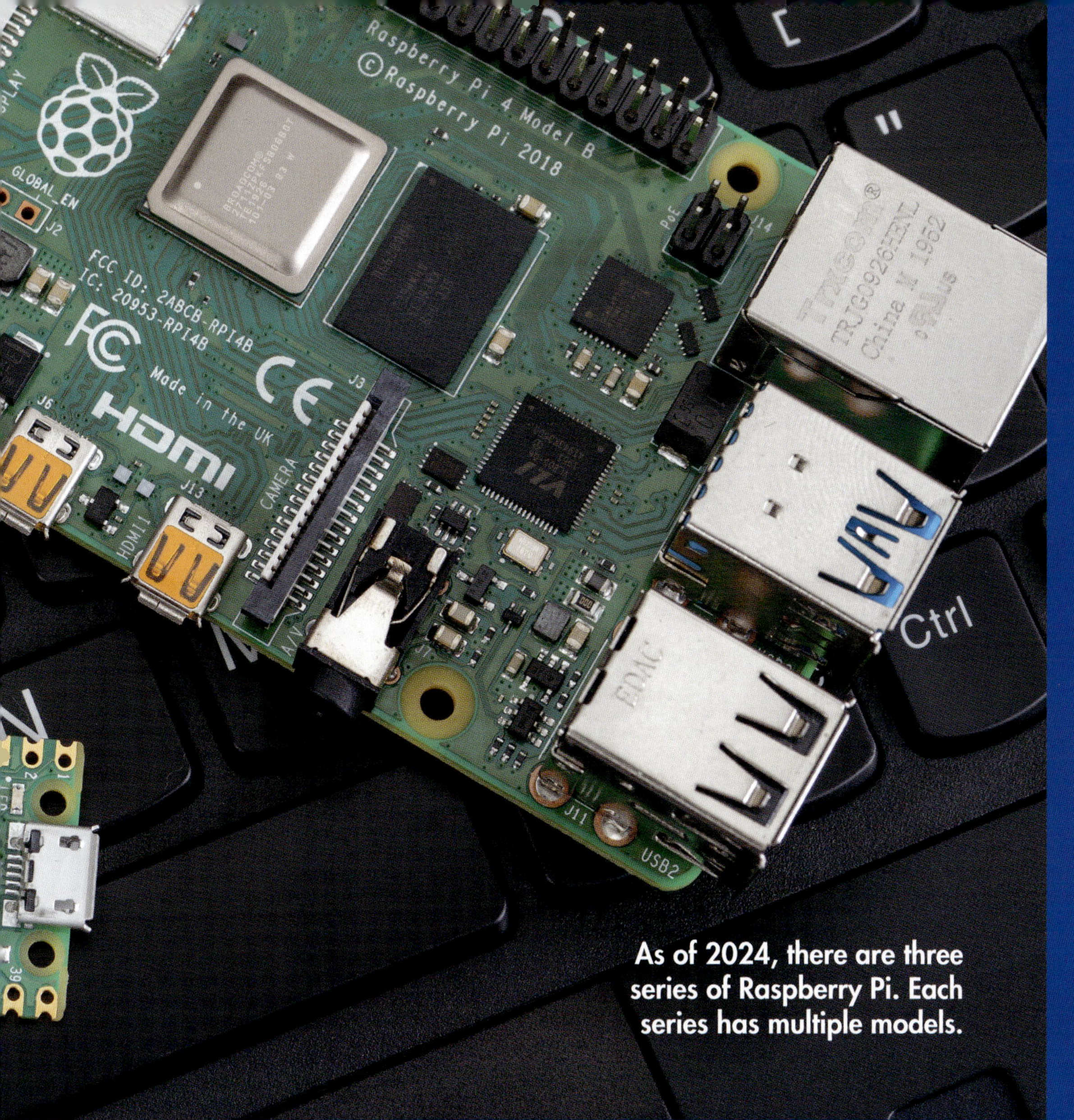

Yes! There are many models of the Raspberry Pi. Some work faster. Some have different ports. You can pick the right one for your project. Newer and faster computers are sure to come!

ASK MORE QUESTIONS

Can I build my own gaming computer?

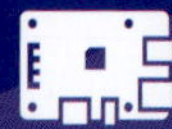

What jobs could I get building computers?

Try a BIG QUESTION: Why do computers need upgrades?

SEARCH FOR ANSWERS

Search the library catalog or the Internet.
A librarian, teacher, or parent can help you.

Using Keywords
Find the looking glass.

Keywords are the most important words in your question.

If you want to know about:
- building a computer, type: GAMING COMPUTER BUILDS
- what jobs use coding, type: CODING JOBS

FIND GOOD SOURCES

Here are some good, safe sources you can use in your research.
Your librarian can help you find more.

Books

Learn Robotics with Raspberry Pi
by Matt Timmons-Brown, 2019.

Raspberry Pi Projects for Kids
by Dan Aldred, 2020.

Internet Sites

Code.org
https://code.org/student/elementary
Learn how to code by playing games.

Kiddle: Raspberry Pi Facts for Kids
https://kids.kiddle.co/Raspberry_Pi
Kiddle is an encyclopedia for kids with facts on many topics. Learn more about Raspberry Pi.

Every effort has been made to ensure that these websites are appropriate for children. However, because of the nature of the Internet, it is impossible to guarantee that these sites will remain active indefinitely or that their contents will not be altered.

SHARE AND TAKE ACTION

Next time an electronic device or toy breaks, don't just throw it away.
See if you can take it apart. Do any of the parts look familiar?

Explore other cool projects online.
Some makers share their designs. Can you understand how it works?

Is there a problem that could be solved with a special robot or device?
Draw your creation and explain how it works.

GLOSSARY

General Purpose Input/ Output pin (GPIO) Pins that send or receive electric signals, without any specified use.

hardware The physical pieces of a computer.

hobby computer A computer you build yourself.

LED Short for light-emitting diode, the lights common in electronics.

motherboard The main circuit board of a computer.

satellite A spacecraft that is sent into orbit around a planet to gather or send back information.

INDEX

coding, 4, 5, 6, 10, 16

General Purpose Input/Output (GPIO) pins, 15

motherboards, 8, 9

names, 6

operating systems (OS), 13

satellites, 17

sizes, 4

Upton, Eben, 6–7

About the Author

Jill Sherman writes books about pop stars, baby animals, and robots. She loves that writing allows her to research and learn about new topics. In addition to writing books, Jill sews her own clothes, creates crossword puzzles, and codes in JavaScript.